Honey Crisp

Jonamac

Pink Lady

Northern Spy

Twenty Ounce

Cortland

Macoun

Me

Winesap

Ida Red

Paula Red

Red Delicious

My grandmother says there's no reason to start
eating apples when peaches are perfect.
So we don't eat the ones that are ready in August.
We eat peaches. Also nectarines.
And plums.

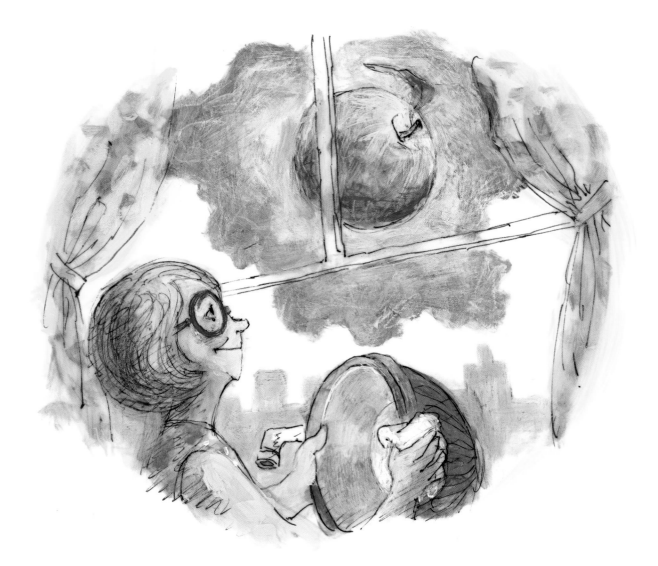

To all the children of Second Street: Delari, Tara, Margo, Garth and Milo
—E.R.L.

For Eden. With gratitude, admiration, and love.
—M.G.

Text copyright © 2009 by Eden Ross Lipson
Illustrations copyright © 2009 by Mordicai Gerstein
Published by Roaring Brook Press
Roaring Brook Press is a division of Holtzbrinck Publishing Holdings Limited Partnership
175 Fifth Avenue, New York, New York 10010

Distributed in Canada by H. B. Fenn and Company Ltd.

Cataloging-in-Publication Data is on file at the Library of Congress
ISBN: 978-1-59643-216-1

Roaring Brook Press books are available for special promotions and premiums.
For details contact: Director of Special Markets, Holtzbrinck Publishers.

First Edition August 2009
Printed in September 2009 in the United States of America
by Worzalla, Stevens Point, Wisconsin
10 9 8 7 6 5 4 3 2

EDEN ROSS LIPSON
APPLESAUCE SEASON
ILLUSTRATED BY **MORDICAI GERSTEIN**

Roaring Brook Press
New York

Applesauce season starts just about the time school opens,
when it is still hot and summery but vacation is over.
One day, Grandma says, "It's time for applesauce."

We live in the city. There are no apple trees, but there are farmers' markets where there are lots of apples. Sometimes my grandmother goes to the market, sometimes my mom and dad go, sometimes my big sisters. If I don't have soccer, I go, too.

I love apple names. In our markets, first come Ida Red and
Paula Red, Twenty Ounce and MacIntosh, Ginger Gold
and Jonagold.

Later there's Macoun, Baldwin, Northern Spy, and King
David, and after that come Winesap and Black Twig and
Mutsu and Mutsu's Mother. And there are lots of others.

We buy six pounds of apples for sauce, because that's just how much our saucepot holds, and we buy as many more for what Grandma calls eating out of hand.

When we get home, the sauce apples are dumped in the kitchen sink and washed. I stand on the stepladder right next to the counter where the grownups chop the apples and choose which ones to cut up first. Sometimes I say put in the little ones, sometimes the big ones, sometimes the dark red or yellow ones.

My grandmother says there have to be at least three kinds in each pot of sauce for real flavor, but sometimes we use more— one of this, and one of that, too. That's why our applesauce is different every week: As one kind of apple disappears another takes its place.

Mom cuts them into quarters, Grandma cuts them into sixths.
I don't know why.

The apples go into the pot, skin, seeds and all. When it is still summer, and there's no cider yet, we add a glass of water or juice, so the apples won't burn when they cook. Later, we add fresh cider.

It doesn't take the apples long to be soft and bubbly and start to smell good.

The first time we make sauce, we make fresh cinnamon sugar,
too. I put sugar into a pretty jar, add some dark brown ground
cinnamon, put the lid on tight, and shake till the sugar turns
pale brown.

When the apples are all soft, a grown-up turns off the stove
and opens the pot to let the mush cool a bit while I go and
get the food mill.

We put the hooks on the bottom of the mill on top of a big
bowl, and carefully put the warm cooked apples into it.
We grind and scrape . . .

. . . grind and scrape, till all the apples have gone through
to the bowl below. All that's left in the mill is a small clump
of the cooked skins and cores and seeds.

Then I put some of the cinnamon sugar into the apples. Not much, just a little. Mom puts in a little slice of butter about the size of the tip of her pinky finger, and Grandma adds a tiny bit of salt.

We taste till it tastes right, and then it cools some more and thickens. Then it's ready.

Daddy doesn't make applesauce. He makes good things to go with it, like potato pancakes or, for special mornings, fancy thin pancakes called crepes.

He puts it with roasts, and if there's any left at the end of the week he uses it in a cake that's very good for snacking.

We celebrate the first sauce of the season. My big sisters and the grown-ups, sometimes the neighbors, too, all sit at the table. We wait until everyone is served—I get a special cup— and then make a good wish for the rest of the season.

We eat applesauce plain, or with ice cream, or cottage cheese,
or gingerbread, or cookies, or sliced bananas.

The color and the thickness and the taste of the sauce changes every single week. Sometimes it's pink and very sweet,

sometimes it's pale brown and a little dry, so we add more cider.

Later, toward Thanksgiving, it's usually yellow.
It is always delicious.

By December there are no more new kinds of apples,
so we stop making sauce and just eat them.

There are other things to do with apples. My grandpa didn't like birthday cake so he always had apple pie. We remember his birthday by having apple pie with ice cream and a candle on top.

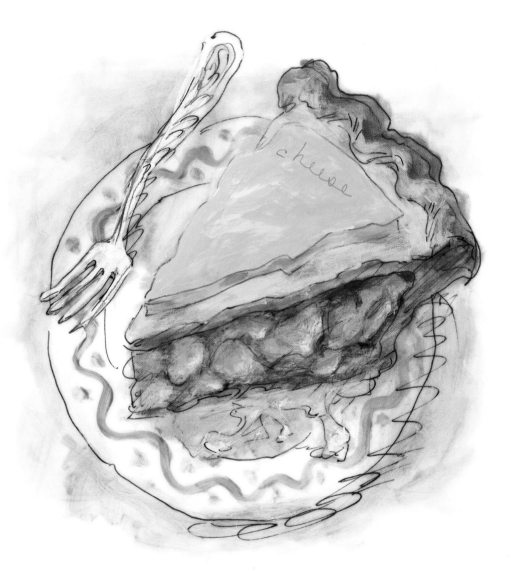

Grandpa always saved a piece of that pie for his breakfast to eat with sharp yellow cheese. Daddy sometimes has that, too.

Apple pie is good, but I still like applesauce best.
Maybe I'll change my mind when I grow up.

Maybe not.

6 lbs. apples, three varieties or more
2 or more cups liquid—water, cider, or juice (or more as needed)
¹/₃ cup cinnamon sugar (or more as needed)
¹/₂ tsp. butter
dash of salt

Optional: If you can find a quince, wash, cut, and add it to the pot.
It will make the sauce pink and sweeter.

Wash and cut up apples and put in a heavy saucepan. Add liquid and cover.
Cook at medium flame until completely soft and foamy—about 20 minutes.

Remove from flame, uncover, and let cool briefly, but while still warm transfer
the apple mixture to a food mill placed over large bowl. Grind down thoroughly.
The sauce will be loose, even runny. It will thicken as it cools. Season to taste.
Serve warm or cold.

My Puppy

Granny Smith

My Grandma

Mutsu

My Mom

Mutsu's Mother

My Dad

MacIntosh

My Older Sister

Ginger Gold

My Other Older Sister

Jonagold